Extra Time

More Poems
by
David Middlewood

Grosvenor House
Publishing Limited

The right of David Middlewood to be identified as the author of this
work has been asserted in accordance with Section 78
of the Copyright, Designs and Patents Act 1988

The book cover is copyright to David Middlewood

This book is published by
Grosvenor House Publishing Ltd
Link House
140 The Broadway, Tolworth, Surrey, KT6 7HT.
www.grosvenorhousepublishing.co.uk

A CIP record for this book
is available from the British Library

Paperback ISBN 978-1-83615-165-4
Hardback ISBN 978-1-83615-166-1

CONTENTS

Section C – Memories

Section D – People and Friends

Section E – Still Loving

Section F – From the Nursing Home and Hope Centre

Section G – In the Waiting Room

PREFACE

Following the publication of my first collection ('It's Time') in 2020, I have been kept busier than ever in terms of writing, especially poetry. Events in and reflections on my daily life continue to prompt me into putting pen to paper (which for me, by the way, is still the first part of the process!) This is often supplemented by requests and commissions to write poems on occasions, events and topics as needed. I have also written several short plays now for the local Hope Centre Drama Group, whilst a local radio station has afforded me regular opportunities to read my poems on air, and talk about poetry and literature.

As before, I am aware that the poems in this collection are of uneven quality, but I console myself with the knowledge that even the best poets, including some of my own favourites such as Hardy, Frost, Wordsworth, Auden, Thomas and Hughes, published material which, shall we say, was well below their best! I am firmly with W.H. Auden when he said that poets should be prepared to write in all forms, whether elegies, sonnets, ballads, eulogies, odes, or any other kinds, including limericks (I actually think I am quite good at limericks, by the way!).

Poetry is not something 'precious', at least not in that particular rather pretentious sense; in other words, all poetry should be 'accessible' -to use Alan Bennett's word-if it is to mean anything to most readers. Poetry takes note of things that are relevant to the readers or listeners, even if they had not thought of them being expressed in such a way before. The reader may say, 'Yes, that IS how I feel' or 'I recognise that-I see what you mean.' If that happens with some of the poems here, I shall be satisfied! Poetry then becomes precious in the real sense of that word-it has certainly been, and still is, a priceless part of my life, bringing me pleasure, solace, insight and hope at different times, depending on the circumstances. As for the title of this collection, 'Extra Time', I believe that is self-explanatory, given that a further five years have elapsed since my previous collection, and that the urge to cherish each living moment as far as possible is something most readers can relate to.

My thoughts and emotions cover many topics, mostly on people in various circumstances, whether it is love, grief, feeling loss, joy or despair. Also of course the poems express the pleasures of such things as gardening, music, writing, attending theatricals and simply helping those more vulnerable than oneself. Although I write very often in the first person, please note that not always does the 'I' refer to me personally! Whether it is a friend trying to describe the experience of playing the piano or, in contrast, living with a loved partner who has developed Alzheimers, I simply try to empathise in those poems with their feelings and thereby perhaps help those in such circumstances. I am grateful to those who tell me that such things do bring them comfort and this to me makes it all worthwhile. Other poems simply give my thoughts about some aspects of modern life!

My own cherished moments are many, and they mostly involve other people, dear friends and family, as well as the natural world. I wish to thank the people at Grosvenor Press for their professionalism, and a good friend, Trish, for her invaluable help in sorting out my manuscript for submission. Above all, of course, I thank my muse, the creator of the majority of the most cherished moments in my life -thank you, Jacqui!

David Middlewood   December 2024

SECTION A – POEMS OF A PANDEMIC

TWO DAYS IN PANDEMIC LOCKDOWN

(In the first week of the first lockdown in March, the Friday was very sunny,
    and the Saturday was grey)
Friday, the sun shone warmly on my back and neck
as I weeded the front garden. The sky was blue,
cloudlessly clear - any fears were far away.
On the pavement someone passed and smiled and waved,
and then another – then another, and each became my brother,
sharing in this unexpected patch of pleasure.
Only when I paused did I become at all aware
of the large dark cloud which I could not see.
Something here was quite unreal.

Saturday, the sun had gone, driven away by cold and grey.
As I gazed at the same plot, I had no zest for digging,
planting; the passers-bys' heads were looking down.
Now in my stomach had been dug a pit,
and I saw too clearly that now darker cloud.
The cold wind chilled my back and neck and, too, my heart
which made me fear that what I'd planted yesterday
might not be seen by me or my new brothers.
Everything was all too real.

I want the sun to come again - I need its warmth;
I want the clear blue sky to help me see again,
clear of clouded thoughts and dark grey fears
of something lurking over there.
I need the business of minor tasks, reminding me of Spring,
hope that comes with watering the newly pushed in bulbs,
the distant words exchanged with someone who'll call out
about the weather or the garden or just - anything!
That sun would keep that big dark cloud at bay
until it comes as Autumn rain – that's real.

HAS NO ONE TOLD THE FLOWERS?

Has no one told the flowers there's a pandemic on?
While a dark cloud hovers over watching thousands die,
my garden shouts with colour, not one grey thing in sight!
The tulips in their blatant red, the hyacinths pink and coy,
waft wantonly towards me in the warming breeze,
like the daffodils and narcissi in yellow and silvery white.
Blossoms on Japanese cherry, on damson and the pear,
they show no sign of holding back; they positively flounce.
Even grape hyacinths, normally restrained and shy,
seem to be profuse, even showy in the grass
shamelessly seeming to be enjoying
their days of limelight in the sun, when I'm nearby.
My mind, already twisted by its failure to make sense
of the weird and tragic scenes around, ones I cannot see,
is tormented by what it is that I don't know is real.
Should I see this startling beauty as a refuge from the storm
or are the flowers just mocking us by saying,
'Look what you've done to us - now see how you feel!'

IN THE GARDEN DURING LOCKDOWN

I sit in my writing room in my garden
and I think in these worrying days
of the people I love and who I hope love me,
because love is what binds us together-two ways;
both in the bond that it makes between them and me,
and in the strength that it gives me to help me believe
that we will recover and get through to the end,
thinking of them all helps this pain to relieve.

I think of them all, my wife, sons and my daughter,
my sister, grandchildren, no longer coming and going.
And I think of my dear friends at care home and Centre
who've brought me such pleasure, through my them knowing .
Though they're 'just up the road', if I cannot meet them,
there's a gap in my life, and a small one in theirs.

This separation, though forced upon us,
will it help us realise our mutual need?
Will it make us resolve to stay closer
when from Covid's prison we're freed?
Stronger family bonding may be the prize
if we can escape—and no one dies.

THE EMPTY CHAIRS

(AT XMAS 2020, AFTER A YEAR OF OVER 60,00 DEATHS IN UK)

Believers and non-believers at Christmas alike this year
may feel the inner urge to utter prayers;
the reason lies around the nation's tables-
those sixty thousand empty chairs.

Each one's a void, a great gap, a loss,
while those in other seats have hearts with space unfilled.
That awful sickening stirring in the stomach's pit,
while the mind cries, 'Gone? No, they were killed!'

A CHRISTMAS LIKE NO OTHER

This Christmas, even non-believers can
all pause at meals and say some prayers
for those who previously shared their joy,
those sixty thousand empty chairs.

While stomachs fill and glasses too,
and background carols fill the air,
we'll think of those who were dragged away,
whose families say, 'It wasn't fair!
Why did the covid pick on them?
They were no worse than you or me.'
And gazing at that empty chair,
just for a moment they can see
that loved one with them there today,
and turning to them, raise a glass
to tell them they won't be forgotten
through all the years that come to pass.

Those of us lucky still to be here,
we owe it to anyone in the empty seat
to do some things better, starting next year,
of twenty twenty there can be no repeat.

A FUNERAL IN LOCKDOWN

The empty cars arrive at the empty chapel;
the empty words float over empty pews.
Most of all, the empty arms outstretch
no one to hold, cry with, or muse
together on the past they've shared.
Only the hearts are full, and full they'll stay
until such time when, gazing at a plaque,
they may find a little of that dead weight slip away.

ATTENDING A FUNERAL IN LOCKDOWN

Empty were the cars that failed to follow the hearse;
there were only the coffin and some flowers.
Empty was the chapel as the coffin lay waiting,
one of many to be fitted in those crowded hours.

Empty were the spoken words for the speakers knew him not,
just another for whom no public tears were shed.
And empty were my aching arms because they could not hold
any fellow mourner to share the fact he's dead.

Only my heart is full, too full for words,
A fullness that perhaps a year from now may ease,
when perhaps we all can stand together by his plaque
and say goodbye, may this aching cease.

JANUARY 2021

(THE FIRST VACCINATIONS)

Always the bleakest, least loved month;
short days, long nights, post festive lethargy-
even February seems a long way off, good grief!
The drizzly clouds and grey that looms
and now not even shop windows' welcoming lights
can offer any temporary relief or hope.

It is dark in here.
It seems hard to find an exit door,
and even then outside for many death has stalked -
and sometimes struck.

And yet? And yet?
A pin-prick of light it CAN be seen-
and if we stare intently we see it slowly spreading out.
like a magic lantern, on to our lives' screens
where we may just see ourselves enacting out
some longed for boring old normality.
Shadows are pushed aside right to the edge
where families are left to weep for those they've lost.
Are we being drugged with hope as this year starts?
Is it possible there'll be a Summer in our hearts?

A SHOT IN THE ARM

I have just been injected with a tiny dose of – hope-
I can feel it coursing through my body's veins.
A hope that out there a Summer waits for us -
only a pin-prick, but I must believe it has scope.

When even Easter seems a long way off, good grief,
in this least loved of months with its wintry gloom,
this pin-prick of light that I've had here today
offers what shuttered shop windows now cannot–relief.

That small dot of light will grow and slowly spread,
like a magic lantern on the screens of all our lives
where we can see ourselves acting out normalities,
until this January's dark has turned to warmth instead.

Though shadows will still lurk within those warmer days,
where families will weep for loved ones that they've lost,
our newly focussed minds help us to want to thank
those who gave the pin-pricks, with our hearts – and praise.

THE 2020 PANDEMIC –
A VIEW FROM 2040

My name doesn't matter - just listen when I say
'My great- grandfather's one hundred today!'
I went to see him –he's still clear and stable,
although physically weaker, mentally so able.
His brain is as sharp and as fresh as the air,
though sometimes his eyes they just seem to stare
into the distance as if he's elsewhere.
So he sat, white haired, in his favourite chair.

We started talking, as I loved him to do,
about his long life and the people he knew.
in his late working days, he'd been an academic,
and I asked him his memories of the great pandemic.
'You mean twenty twenty?' I nodded. His look
was of someone who had just opened a book,
a book of great meaning that meant something dear,
and I think on the edge of his eye was a tear.
Suddenly, I saw that he was old and his tears
were for what he had lost throughout all the years.

After he'd cleared a lump in his throat,
he then spoke quite sharply, which made me take note.
'We were fools,' he said firmly. 'We were idiots all.
Let me see now, dear, what I can recall.
It started in China; though we never found out
exactly how far it had spread, there's no doubt
that they closed down their cities and soon, as by fate,
it went off in Italy, in its northern state.
In England, we heard of the deaths and, as they grew,
when Spain and France followed, we knew we were due.

I had family in Greece and Australia too -
I was a typical member of the whole global crew!
'We're all in it together'- that was the phrase-
but I tell you this - they were frightening days!

Well now, the first days of the lockdown were funny.
The weather, you see, was all blue skies and sunny.
I worked in the garden, planting bulbs and seeds,
and smiled at those passing as I pulled up the weeds.
I waved at these passing, first one then another,
and somehow I felt that each one was my brother.
The whole situation was normal but unreal,
like being in a film, and yet you could feel
that somewhere out there was trouble to be,
like a big black cloud, only one you can't see.

Then as days passed, and the death figures rose,
you began to feel frightened and began to suppose
that your family and friends you might see no more.
Sometimes you felt someone had closed a door
on the whole outside world, while you hid in your bed,
but of course you kept going on living instead.
Some days you pretended and some you just lied,
there were days when great Grandma just sat down and cried.
Mostly she was wonderful, always beautiful to see,
she cooked all the meals and was loving to me.

Then we heard of a friend living in the same street,
how she'd caught the virus via some she'd had to meet.
We had met her and hugged her just a few days before,
but now she'd recovered, so this gave us some more
hope, not just for us but for so many others,
sons, daughters, grandchildren, sisters and brothers.
Then we heard awful news from a care home quite near,
where we'd visited and made some friends very dear;
three of the ladies that we'd known really well,
had died from the virus, as from some ghastly spell.

That awful virus, in their lungs it had crept,
when we heard that they'd gone, we both broke down and wept.
Even worse was, we knew, we could not say goodbye,
not go to a funeral or service, or even stand by
a grave or a headstone or share memories with a friend–
what a miserable way for their sweet lives to end!'

The old man he paused; I squeezed his hand as I stood.
'Was there anything remembered in any way good?'
After an effort, his face eased into a smile,
not one of happiness, but one that says while
there is suffering, there is always a chink
of hope that amidst pain makes you think
that somewhere out there could be a light ray
that will break through the dark and shine on us one day.

'Well, yes,' he said. 'One thing my mind sees
is a park full of daisies, and blossom on trees.
The grass being uncut, the flowers simply spread;
when you sat on the grass, it was like being in bed
in a land full of whiteness – it lifted your soul
and it made me feel once again I was whole,
with that pit in my stomach being lifted away,
and somewhere in the future was a better day.
What else? Well, the friendship, people's loving care;
the way that everyone was willing to share.

Oh, yes, and the wild life, perhaps that most of all.
More birds in the garden, and now I recall,
a squirrel, a hedgehog, using gardens to roam -
it was as if they felt they were sharing our home.
I liked to think such creatures had come to reclaim,
and I'd hoped that, after, it could stay just the same.
Perhaps that's the thing that we learned most of all,
that our abuse of the earth had led us to a fall.

We'd become so obsessed with our goods and our wealth,
we'd thought that THINGS mattered more than our health;
our emotions and minds we'd closed off for high tech,
all to make our lives easier and it brought us to wreck
this world that's so lovely and natural, full of plenty -
we were paying the price in that year, twenty twenty.'

Great-grandfather paused, I could see he was weary.
'You'd better go home now,' he said in as cheery
a voice as he could manage to muster.
'We don't want your parents getting all in a fluster!'
So I gave him a hug and a kiss, and I left.
But when I got home, I felt somehow bereft.
Though I'd learned so much from what I'd been told,
I'd also lost something and I felt I'd grown old.

Late that night, Mum came in with a face like the grave.
'Now listen, my darling, I want you to be brave'.
I could tell by her look that she'd recently cried -
'I have got to tell you – Great-grandfather's died!'

SECTION B – TIME PASSES

LEARNING

I learned laughter when I was a boy
- from my mother dropping a wayward stitch,
and clipping my ear with a grin -
from my sister hitting a cheering lad,
who urged on my racing rival to win.

I learned smiling when I was a lad
- at my father's filthy wartime songs,
because laughing could not be allowed-
at my plump friend's attempts to keep up with me,
though inside I felt he was proud.

I learned crying when I was a man
- at the loss of my mother whom I failed
to thank her enough for my life -
- at the thought of losing the woman
who'd take my smiles with her, my wife.

UNDUSTED

Although the past does not exist, it is always present,
and we need it - for memory can set us free.
We know the lies we told ourselves – and others too -
the self-deception in the face we showed the world at times,
but, looked at through the lens of memory, truth can set us free,
free from what we said we knew,
compared with what we really knew -
and so the dust of then can be now blown away.
Yet should it be?
Most relics have their value in being what they are,
antiques remaining as they were in times past.
Why should we shine and polish them for viewing for today?
Does not then their value drop?

The memories of childhood are ones free from dust -
the antique clock upon the wall,
the jasper vase on the sideboard,
the mother's thimble on the table.
These gather no dust but, though no longer physically tended,
they shine with all the lustrous dullness
as if it were yesterday that I saw them in their place.

But wasted years they must be left all undisturbed,
a whole decade of dust upon them
with just an odd shaft of light piercing through to show a new born baby.
Or even two decades perhaps?
Or is it simply that these other years have had less time to gather dust?
Only the future can tell -
and the future does not exist, no more than does the past.

As when we open up an old book and find a flower pressed within,
and when you try to grasp it, it collapses
and disintegrates in all its frailty and falls apart,
leaving you wondering why you did not leave the pages closed
and the flower intact for someone else perhaps,
who might even cherish what you would destroy.
So memory can set us free -
if left undisturbed, we can select what is our best,
whilst leaving what we will -
those old relics serve no purpose for us now -
perhaps they never did.

And now free, we find we have come full circle
and we can busily shape our own memories
as new yesterdays speed by.
These new memories, so quickly old, have no time to gather dust
because each day they are the now,
because their past and future do not exist.
As now, I sit in sunlight in the garden,
surrounded by poppies red and pink,
by clematis blue and jasmine yellow,
whilst human love grows in the house,
knowing that tomorrow,
when today does not exist in this form any more,
its memory is almost real
and I am free to live with it.

WHO NEEDS WORDS?

'Besmirched', 'bespoken', and 'bespattered',
How I love such words from an age no longer here!
You can taste them in your hungry mouth
and hear them challenging your eager ear.
You can see them living on the page or sheet
while you battle to find their personal beat.
They can paint a picture with emphatic lines,
rooting themselves in what is real and seen;
the old masters hewed each one to fit its use,
drawing on what was then and now has been.

I hate the U and LoL of this world's words;
The pared down puniness of their often petty way.
They have no power to let us see how users feel,
though proving their use for those craving power per se.
The reason for our loss, it's always said, is speed.
We must go faster; there's no time to waste on words.
We must have paperless offices and cashless banks;
rather like twitterers with no time for actual birds!
Stepping off an HS2, thirty minutes nearer to the grave,
will they know what to do with all this time they save?

A BOWER FOR EVERYONE

Two crab apples I've bent them over into one,
forming an arch which grew into a kind of bower.
And beneath, two facing seats just made for two as one,
so, often we sat for minutes, or sometimes hour on hour.
And in those times, over tea, or just occasionally wine,
the world was changed and everything made quite clear,
all its great issues, along with family, and art, and friends,
the universe turned over and around and back to here.

And when at last we move indoors and finally to sleep,
Then find tomorrow that the world's about the same,
should we despair and see that time as wasted,
watching politicians and popsters shout for power and fame?
Their empty noise drowns out what all we humans seek-
black or white, Asian or East, straight or trans or gay -
our own bower where we all can sit and speak
and listen to what others may have to say.
If found, sometimes we'd silent sit, free from bitter strife,
knowing that what makes up all our common life
are moments like these, mostly small, intense and real,
so all our differences become the same in how we feel.

BIG QUESTIONS – SMALL ANSWERS

After two hours of concentrated toil,
I look proudly at the restored garden patch,
still with disorder, but with gloss removed,
and think that that was time well spent.
Satisfying and fulfilling work it was – and then -
all at once into my head
comes a train of thought, instead
of satisfaction comes a doubt
that I struggle to keep out -
those were two hours of my life's millions
and what have they really done for others?

Along with awareness that it needs to be repeated
in a year or less, I'm sure, come the questions -
How have I made the world a better place?
How have I benefitted the wider race?
Is all this futile, lacking meaning?
Just when my thoughts are that way leaning
a robin hops happily into this new domain,
coming within inches of my hand – approvingly.

Is it telling me, in some small way, I've made things better,
perhaps contributed to something bigger?
Removing gloss, I've let rough beauty emerge
and both of us have a better chance
to share in a future such as this might be.
I think I can find meaning in this tiny deed
and perhaps help others to find theirs too -
for it was all done with love, for love,
and that's as much as any of us can do.

NEVER ASK HOW LONG

When the first snowdrop pushes its head through
defying the bleakness of January's grey,
never think or, worst still, say
'But you will soon be gone away'
Feed on its whiteness which it shares with you.

When tulips start to parade their summer show,
bringing glamour in yellow and pink,
please never for one moment think
'They'll be gone before we blink!'
Embrace them as the friends you love and know.

When real love at last enters your life for real,
transforming you both in strange ways,
never ask for how many weeks or days
can this state continue to amaze.
Soak up each second of this thing you feel.

If you don't relish life when you get it
It'll be gone and you'll regret it!

IN MY GARDEN

Sometimes if I close my eyes,
I wonder where I am.
I can smell the orange jasmine and,
even with eyes closed, I can see
the damson blossom shimmering
above the multi-coloured tulips
and yellow wallflowers.
I am in my garden and now, when I look
at my hands, I can see my fingers
covered with the dirt
that makes all that smell and that shimmer.

When my fingers push into the soil,
they feel things I cannot find elsewhere.
As well as worms and bugs, dead leaves,
and stuff that rots away for good,
they find some trigger in my brain
that switches off concerns and questioning,
giving me access to what I feel,
and satisfaction that I know what's real.

THE ALLOTMENT PEOPLE

They cut and they dig and they hoe and rake;
their bodies strain and their muscles ache,
and when they groaningly stretch high,
almost hearing their backbones sigh
with relief, they can rest on their hands
and take in the continent of separate lands.
Of these of course they rule just one-
it's the weirdest mixture of toil and fun.

But, more than that, they see above their heads
the sky which across all the same world spreads;
sometimes, through a cloud-rift, they glimpse the sun,
sparing them a few seconds on its global run
It passes, they return as everyone must do
to the daily world peopled by me and you
to manage their own world as they stoop to see
if they have enough beans to take home for tea.

BON VOYAGE

(TO A COUPLE SETTING OUT TO TRAVEL THE WORLD)

As you set out on this life's dreamed of travels,
we hope you find what you look for as time unravels.
You'll cross new frontiers and meet new faces
increase your knowledge of countries and races.
Some days when you wake in a strange Asian dwelling,
you'll think of the stories that you will be telling
on your return to the world that you know,
which you'll then see with new eyes, your faces aglow.
You'll have found new foods, new smells and new tastes,
no things that are first found can be seen as wastes.
But most of all you will find something that's old,
something you've had with you through time untold,
you'll find yourselves, who you really are, and where,
each one for yourself, and - with love - as a pair.

A WEDDING AT THE GUILDHALL, NORTHAMPTON

Many's the ceremony that's been crafted here
in this old building, several added, year on year.
As trivial as we are, like bricks, each one a tiny part
of the history of this place, long long before our start
and long after we have gone, the building will persist
in witnessing more lovers, as 'Just married' couples kissed.

It's easy your own small part in this long tale to dismiss;
but time was watching as you took that kiss.
A hundred years from now, when someone comes to gaze around,
and cares to look beyond mere physical surround,
they will find into their soul will steal
an understanding of what happened here today, and feel
just as this couple did in times then past,
that what was felt and said in here today will last.

I like to think that here when future couples wed,
and some of those past rites once more being said,
that a tiny fragment of what most of us call love
flies up to the rafters, settling high above,
and looks down on couples' exchanging eyes,
ready to collect the next piece as it upward flies.

CHANGE AND NO CHANGE

Once the problem was rationing, today it's the waste;
today it's four courses, back then was fish paste.
From black and white telly to delivery drones,
from chips wrapped in paper to micro-chip phones;
we don't mend our clothes, we just buy some others;
we don't have our hand-me-downs from sisters or brothers.
We're living much longer, diseases get cured;
along comes a new bug; our resistance is skewered.
We've got more millionaires than ever before-
and more homeless people who have to sleep on the floor.

Everything changes, some for better, some worse;
I suppose that's the theme of this little verse.
Sometimes you might think that the world has gone mad;
it can't make up its mind what is good and what's bad.
But when I see a small child with an old cardboard box
making a cave out of sheets and odd socks,
lost in a world they themselves have created,
you feel that this truth just has to be stated,
that whatever the changes and whoever's to blame,
perhaps underneath, people ARE still just the same.

THE MAGIC OF RADIO

At my command, a whole world is there,
where I'm in control, and I don't have to share.
Music, drama, politics, or just news and chat,
the radio gives me every bit of that .

When I turn that dial with a satisfying click,
I'm into a world that's informal yet slick;
It's somewhere where I can be in control,
if I want test cricket, I can follow each ball.

Maybe it's music, some for every taste,
non-stop provision, not a moment to waste;
Beatles to Beethoven, from jazz to hip-hop-
we are spoilt for choice, like an ever-open shop.

For the earlier risers, to help start the day,
there are cheery comperes to get you on your way.
For late night listeners, there's music to sooth
presented by deejays, epitome of smooth.

And then for the drivers, whether woman or man,
whether they're driving a car or a van,
an estate or a lorry, a mini or a cab,
if they get bored, there's this dial they can grab,
and then they're transported, via their destination,
to another world that they reach through a station.

For many, local radio is their joy and pride,
where they can tune in to their trusted and tried.
There are weather reports, sometimes quite jolly,
So you can decide if it's sunhat or brolly.
There are traffic reports, keeping right up to date,
to help you to check to avoid being late.
There's lots of music of course you can hear being played
for local listeners as they ply their trade.

The bonus of radio, unlike the TV,
where you always have to keep looking to see,
is you hear all this magic while you carry on
doing whatever you've started upon.

You can be doing the ironing, or washing a floor,
or putting a new coat of paint on a door,
changing a light bulb or trimming a hedge,
peeling potatoes or cooking some veg.
Or you could be at work as a cabinet maker,
making some cakes or buns as a baker,
a tiler or tailor, hairdresser or barber
striving to give clients the look that that they harbour.

An ambler, a gambler who loses or wins,
or those brilliant people who empty our bins;
stuck in the office, battling red tape,
the radio offers a form of escape.

So, whoever you are, doctor, patient or nurse,
whatever you're doing, I hope you won't curse,
For now I can tell you, for better or worse,
I've finally come to the end of my verse!

AMATEUR THEATRICALS

Amateur theatricals – oh, what larks!
In village halls or in public parks,
church halls, school halls – almost anywhere -
if a space is available, you'll find them there.

These heroes and heroines put on their plays,
with performances over two, three or four days.
Comedies, mysteries, pantos and farces,
they give them their all as every year passes.
Retired or working, female or male,
these part-time thespians can tell you a tale
of evenings spent in sharing a laugh,
before it's down to the pub to have a swift half.
But also of toiling at coming in on cue,
or mislaying your script – later found in the loo!
Grappling with a word that you can't seem to get right,
putting on a wig in which you look such a sight!

Oh, those winter evenings, out in the dark,
wondering if you'll ever be up to the mark,
emerging from rehearsal after learning that line,
to find out that your car's got a parking fine!
And what about at home when you're learning your role?
Driving family mad till they're tired of the whole
wretched business-'Don't know why you took it on!
Why can't you play bingo or darts or mah-jong?!'

Think back to the casting – what part would you get?
And will we EVER finish painting that set?
Who can play grannies? We're too old for teens!
Sometimes you wonder just what it all means!
Until the time comes – the show must go on!
The butterflies surge as your costumes you don.
You think for a moment that you might take flight-
but then you recall - it's all right on the night!

And when it's all over - and the set has come down,
you return to normality – perhaps with a frown -
you realise you'll miss it the following week,
but glad at the same time you've no lines to speak.
You say 'Never again! Let someone else do it!'
And yet after days with your mind going through it,
you finally admit to yourself that you're hooked,
no matter how silly you felt the last time you looked.
So you go to auditions for the very next show,
hoping to be something that you really know
will contribute in some way to the whole thing,
and praying that in your part, you won't have to sing!

But, whether you're prompting or playing the lead,
or just selling programmes, you're filling a need-
a need that we all have -to be entertained.
And in watching the show we feel that we've gained
something special that we didn't have before
and so the very next time that you open that door,
those folk will be there-they love your shows-
for this is the truth that everyone knows-
amateur drama is really great fun,
bringing joy and fulfilment to everyone!

THE POWER OF HOPE

I used to think that hope was passive,
something we sat with while we waited,
either with expectations low,
or more urgently with our breath baited.

But since those stands of August Seven,
when millions stood for hour on hour
to thwart the thugs and call for peace -
we all learned that hope is power.

Not that power that likes rule over others
or takes pleasure in that, even pride,
but the power of knowing that everywhere
with all of us, hope's on our side.

Some need a hope just to get through the day,
perhaps just a sign that somebody cared-
and these genuine protests showed us this-
that hope's more powerful when it's shared.

This country and its communities
showed then that they can more than cope.
In the varied faces of each person there,
shone the unifying force of hope.

So let's turn that shared hope into deeds,
show that hatred's venom we can weather.
Compassion. Justice, love WILL win
when we that hope all act together.

BELONGING

Like indigenous races who came before we so-called settlers did,
the creatures of this piece of land that I have always called our garden
they tell and show me of belonging to the land, and not the other way.
I'll try to keep my side of the bargain, the way our ancestors bid.

The new birds' nests each Spring, the earthworms delving deep,
the crab apples rotting in the ground, the bumblebees and butterflies,
the countless ants and spiders, even hedgehogs, squirrels and frogs
will help me ease my guilt at what's been done; perhaps more easily I'll sleep.

The blackbird supervises me as I try belatedly to make amends
by letting grasses grow and building insect houses and bug homes;
he seems to wonder, though I've started on the quest, about my legacy
for his and my children, in our work together -he knows it never ends.

ALWAYS LIKE THIS?

The year is twenty thirty and the family pause to stay.
The adults sit and mop their brows as the sun beats down,
while two children chase around the square,
ignorant of the heat and the dust that's there.
The parents move along the bench to find their ease,
and gain more shade from the two crab apple trees
that form the archway above their heads.
The father idly asks the girl to mind the thorns
on the hawthorn hedge
which frames one edge
of this welcome oasis on a sweltering day.

'Good job it's here', one of them is heard to say;
the other nods as if it could be any other way.
They never wonder was it always thus;
why should they when it's there for them?
Today's always today and yesterdays are gone-
why should or could they know
of what brought this square to show
its present state they welcome so.

The toil and trouble that turned this place
into what it is today as it shows its face.
The new friendships formed, at least one or two,
the spirit of togetherness that prospered through
the clearance of the site that had been so abused.
It's right that history is no longer there
leaving new locals to enjoy this square.
But wait! - a young child spots a brass plaque on the wall,
and hesitantly reads its words which do recall
those things of a decade back.
And we ourselves can fully track
it all simply by friendships
which persist today
long after the rubbish was first cleared away.

SANTA FROM WITHIN

Cocooned inside my red and fluffy white,
I see the true side of our youngest race.
Their eyes they really shine, their voices rise
as they meet one of their dreams face to face.
'And when you come to me,' they say,
'I'll be asleep but that's alright.
I know you'll leave me what I've asked
downstairs beside the fireplace in the night.'

What moves me most though is their wish
to be as kind to me as I could dream,
with endless offers of mince pies and milk,
and carrots for all the reindeer team.
And when one tells me he'll leave for me
any prize he wins in raffle or a draw,
I can forgive myself not really being him
when I take off the red and fluffy white I wore.

A SENSE OF PURPOSE

Watching my small child in the living room
as he pursues a bright orange balloon,
I muse on his single-mindedness,
the sucked-in cheeks, the frowning eyes,
the purpose in his moving feet,
oblivious to me in his blindness.

Son of mine, I pray you lose,
as you grow to independence,
this dangerous determination
that's recommended for success in life;
a sense of purpose, one ambition,
that's only gained by constant application.

My son, do you think I should be here,
having found myself to be the who I am,
if I had kept that singlemindedness?
Instead I found an openness of heart
which let another in who helped me find
myself and thus all others too.

MY PEN AND I

There's something reassuring about a pen,
especially when you know each other well.
So when I want to share a feeling or some thoughts,
I reach for the pen,
and as my fingers clasp around its stem
it's as if I am already clasping them.

The words are writing out themselves upon the sheet
without much pause it seems to me,
so when I look back on what they've said,
so says the pen!
When I read what it is has said that day,
it's always what I'd meant to say!

Is it because the pen can smoothly flow
just like my thoughts and feelings move,
like some continuous spidery web-
unceasing pen.
Does it know my thoughts, outer and under?
Am I leading or following, I often wonder!

As it moves across the page,
it seems more concerned with what's ahead
than what it may have left behind,
the trail of pen,
until it finds there's nothing more to say,
so it stops, ready to be tucked away.

So, when we both are done, my pen and I,
and we can leave the scene both fulfilled,
not really bothering whether there'll be reply
to me and pen.
Until the next time something stirs my heart
then on our next trip together we both may start.

TWO KINDS OF HOMELESS

I meet, read and rage about the homeless and poor,
and talk with so many who sleep in a door.
Then I read of the rich with their five different places,
the five minute celebs with their orange-peel faces.
and I'm angry till I realise in one way they're the same-
it's just that they're caught on a treadmill of fame.
Some may have five houses but do they have a home?
A place where you go to when too tired to roam?
No matter the cost, style, materials or size,
home isn't somewhere you can judge by your eyes.
A home isn't something that you have to earn-
you walk into somewhere, your stomach may churn.
You know it knows you and you've passed its test-
then it wraps itself round you - forget all the rest!

STORING MOMENTS

I want to bottle such moments as these -
- as when the sun is warm upon my head,
and I seem to actually feel the greenness of the leaves,
    whilst the wallflowers' oranges and browns
vie with the tulips' showy yellow and red
for my attention - they all hold me there -
all of us bound together as this warmth we share
-and then uncork them when it's hard to see
anything but the darkness of a newsy noisy world
which threatens to blot out the sun
and come between such things and me.

I want to wrap such moments up –
-as when my fingers feel the buddleia's rough bark,
and I see my nails dirty while I move a stone
to let a daisy underneath begin to breathe,
knowing that this afternoon at least I've made my mark
so I smile for the tiny celandine
opening its petals as it pushes up through the path
-and carefully unwrap them when I can't escape
the truth of what my kind is self-inflicting
through greed and rivalry and squabbles over space,
leading to wars, starvation, genocide and rape.

I want to put these moments in a box-
-as when I stretch up to the sun to ease my ache,
thinking there's not much more contentment I could take,
my mind still with my dearest friends I left an hour past
and knowing inside the house is the one love that will last,
yet still I hear a passer-by call out an Easter greeting
whilst a bumble bee settles beside me for our meeting -
-so that I can lift the lid and show all this
to my current mind and more so to my heart,
perhaps to offset in some small way another crime
we've all committed on the world of which this all is part.

PASSING THROUGH

(REFLECTIONS IN 2024 ON SPENDING FORTY YEARS IN A HOUSE BUILT IN 1857)

I pause to wonder what the labour's worth,
mopping my brow after the latest tiny task,
and weighing all our changes in the scales of time
how permanent will my new work be, I ask,
when the next ones passing through arrive.

Of course, in doing all I can to better things,
I sometimes take them back into their past;
that seventies paved garden at the front,
in these green days, I could not let that last
and now bright flowers bloom once more.

We get other glimpses of how things were,
like a patch of wallpaper behind the fridge,
or a garish paint beneath a sober layer.
Such things uncovered give a bridge
into the moods of others making marks.

Some things I do get the house's approval.
as I arrange my Dickens' novels on the shelf,
I get a sense of someone saying it's fine,
as if the great man were here himself,
seeing the house and he were of one time.

Likewise I bring from my forties boyhood home
my old bedtime candlestick holder.
When it finds its place, I feel the house's smile
as we both now are some seventy years older,
and we can continue living together now.

Through two world wars and a recent pandemic,
this place has weathered and mostly thrived;
even the front iron railings resisted the call
for wartime meltdown and so they survived.
Like us, they wobble but will last a little longer.

The dead feet of the past here tread so softly,
and when I brush against the old back garden wall,
and finger and fondle the crevices and gaps,
I seem to hear past generations as they call
with kindness that I'll be joining them soon.

This house and us we understand each other;
it knows of course that we shall go first
not with any sense of triumph or sorrow,
just aware that we humans are cursed
to be those who are just passing through.

So are we merely like discarded lovers,
cast aside when our mutual affair has ended?
Or does our love for each other in this place
mean that we have been here befriended
by this house as our watchful guardian?

We've planted some trees here that will last;
even new owners will see the worth of these,
though they'll cast so much else as old- fashioned
in a desperate desire some new mode to please.
Trees have a habit of growing on people!

We've both lived in properties but this is our home;
we plan to end here, though one may go before.
The one child we brought into the world here
was our new love that grew more and more.
Only this house knew and shared it with us.

What counts is the life we have lived here,
more than high ceilings or the cellar below;
one day the house will wave gently goodbye;
and welcome newcomers – who, we won't know.
After all, we were just passing through.

WHY ARE THEY SO AFRAID OF SILENCE?

Why are so many so afraid of silence?
It is in silence that we find ourselves,
as there's nothing between us and the truth.
We are as naked as were Adam and Eve
when all they had around them to believe
were themselves and what they saw and felt.
Yet today so many put around them a kind of belt
of noise of twenty-four seven hour humming.
Are they afraid of their own second coming?

It's been in silence I've found someone, the real me,
the good, the bad, the many in-betweens,
and having found that person, lost since teens,
I found I could clearly hear the sounds of silence
in all the many forms they take,
like bird song while nests they make,
like truth in loving vows, not fake,
and most of all, for pure human nature's sake,
the value of this life and what it means simply to be.

SECTION C – MEMORIES

BOYHOOD FRIENDS

'And did you hear that Barry Henlow's died?'
My sister asks at a catch-up call.
When I reply he seemed okay
the last time he and I had met,
and she points out that sixty years
gives lots of time for folk to change(!),
I realise how deep some memories are set.

For he's still part of my childhood and youth,
just one small vivid part of my mind's album.
Behind closed eyes, they are all still there-
the Maurices, the Alans, the Peters and the Roys.
Different every one, yet every one the same,
featuring in familiar scenes long played out
in the rough and ready rusticity of boys.

Before girls came along to break us into pairs,
football sides, and skates on pond, and wobbly bikes,
were the only real things outside home and school.
Any girls who joined us in those innocent years
were really boys of slightly different make,
who, in skirts, couldn't seem to kick or throw a ball,
and numbered creepy crawly things among their fears.

But what of closer ones, as Allen, Doug and John?
The ones with whom we swap cards December time,
whom when we meet every two decades or so,
pick up from where we left just as before.
They still most vividly are seen as then they were,
in that youthful scrapbook of my mind,
though more than three centuries we have, we four!

And when I will be told that one of these so dear
has 'passed on', I'll feel the pain, the loss;
and even if I'm present at their very last goodbye,
I know, eyes closed, I'll still see him as child or youth.
Or should it be that I'm first to be the one
about whom the news comes - 'He's no more,'
they'll feel the same, for we all share one truth-
-that I won't be dead to them, nor them to me.
We will live on, not ageing in their or my mind's eye
until the last of all of us has left from here.
Those who'll remain only remember us from later days,
and, perhaps looking at some faded black and whites,
may say, 'I wonder were they ever young?
Why did they in those times look so old always?'

INTRUSIONS

An ordinary day, with routine stuff.
Sees his mother's grave.
Recalls all that she gave,
Nothing left to save -
and weeps he never thanked her enough.

Dusting frames on the wall above her,
her father's photo she cleans,
recalls childhood scenes,
asks what it all means,
and in tears asks out loud did he love her.

A name in a book-her mind flies-
disowned baby she'll see;
only way to be free
to die young of TB.
She wonders where else were there lies.

These past moments, painful and keen,
dark fancies they feed,
to dusty corners they lead;
do they answer a need?
Without dirt, we don't know what is clean.

TRITE PHRASES

Trite phrases such as 'secret affair' and 'amour',
they have their place in many a person's past.
But their triteness takes on a real solidity
when what was found there comes to last.

If I close my eyes, I still can see eyes looking up at me,
just caught in the half-light of a dull night.
I feel your warmth and feel the strength of love
in your not so strong arms around me-it has to be!
The rain beats remorselessly on a car's roof;
what is it telling us? Go back or go on?
We hear its message and feel its wildness
accentuating the warmth of the coupleness
inside the car that is for now our world.
As the rain eases and I stand outside adjusting
to all that's new. I look across the land of puddles
and I feel a surge of thrill at what is now ours,
those desert wastes and icy arctic spaces!
We have entered new worlds, my love, and they are ours
where trite phrases have their place with us
because we have made the things themselves for real.

THE DESERTER

I only remember his tired ashen face
and the flicker of relief when they came.
I thought the men in red caps were his friends-
they all walked close together when they left.
Mum said he was only a boy,
and she'd made him a cup of tea
when she'd found him in the Anderson
that Autumn of forty three .
Perhaps she'd thought of her brother abroad,
or of me, four years old, with no dad.
I remember her grip on my shoulder
And the wet in her eyes for that lad.

Of the thousands that flit through our lives,
nameless, momentary, then gone,
just a few we recall, like that runaway boy,
and their whole lives we speculate on.
Shipped off and turned into a hero?
Or killed in the last year of war?
Celebrating the big hundred right now?
Or most of his life just a bore?

I can only think of his bloodless face
and imagine his gut-wrenching fear;
I think I'm glad he followed his feelings-
and I'd tell him so, were he now here.

THE TREE BEYOND THE CLASSROOM

Across the flat top of the engineering block.
where slender windows show the shining bulbs inside,
I can see,
And there's a tree that's bothering me.

I mean it bothers me because I can't describe its colour;
it's a kind of gold and brown and yellow and rust
and you know
that tree is really baffling me.

The ruthless glutted clouds surge by with sombre speed
while a stab of sunlight fires the tree for me.
I tell you,
that tree is really worrying me.

Inside this classroom there is order-each knows his place.
I know that what these scratching pens produce
I'll score them
but we can't begin to reach that tree.

Perhaps I'll take these youngsters out to see the tree,
And write a poem or prose about it in their books.
Then you'll see – maybe -
that tree it will no longer frighten me.

HARVEST TIME

Along the hedge I see the Combines hard at work
lifting their dinosaur heads to grasp and chomp.
Across a gate I watch the yellowy mass of corn
spewed out as castles on a golden beach.

Sadly I think of how that beach will turn
to a smouldering wasteland as its remnants burn.
The winter's wildness will make the whole field black;
surely, I feel, the corn cannot come back.

But then at once I find I realise
how long ago men here with scythes
those same doubtings they may have felt,
as swathe by swathe their blows they dealt-
and yet the tide of corn still ripples here,
awaiting as the dinosaurs draw near.

I leave the gate-the combines still have fields to go.
I need not fear the winter now that I know
that when in future Augusts someone passes near,
the harvesters – or offspring – will be here,
and that someone else will, in both sun and rain,
repeat my words, 'It's harvest time again.'

WAITING AND HOPING

She had not come.
I waited, waited, and my mind grew numb.
Excuses floated in the gloomy air
wrapping their flimsiness around the fact she was not there.
The shifty feet and stupid smile
were all my role could offer in a style
to show the passers-by I did not care.
Until then unannounced, the agreed hour
suddenly told it all from the fateful tower.
I meanfully muttered as it tolled its sum;
but the truth remained – she had not come.

Ten minutes more, as decreed by hope,
when even my watched hand seemed to mope,
then – a breathless gasping in my ear,
sighing out, 'I'm here! I'm here!'
Turning, and peering through a teary storm,
I saw a face now taking its familiar form.
Only half hearing some tale of something 'late',
and of fearing something of a failing to wait,
we moved away, knowing we'd more than cope,
the four of us – she and I, and love and hope.

A RAINY SUNDAY

Always the worst day, Sunday,
especially when the weather is foul.
Outside the rain beat relentlessly
and the wild wind rose into a howl.
'No chance of a bus trip to town today,
just to have something to do',
he mutters as he prepares the lunch,
inadvertently laying for two.
The main food carefully pre-prepared,
he waits while the vegetables cook,
and stares at the steamed-up window
whilst knowing it's useless to look.

Not a soul can inhabit the world outside;
what mortal would do so in such rain?
And yet, through the shrieking tumult,
he hears a tap tap tap on the pane.
Wiping the steam from the glass in his face,
he peeps out at the chaotic storm;
does he hear her say, 'It's lonely out here
in this cold, while you're there in the warm.
When I left you, after years together,
it was right I was buried so deep.
But I'm lonely here now without you
and I need you where we both can sleep.'

Forgetting the meal in the making,
he unlocks and opens the door,
letting in the rain as he peers outside
and puddles form on the floor.
No sign of her or any other
can be seen in the gathering gloom;
only the branch of a sycamore tree
can be seen by the light from the room.
With each gust, it knocked at the window,
he sees now as he stares into space;
but surely that voice was familiar and real
- and did he imagine that face?

So he stands still in the doorway,
transfixed by the past getting cold,
should he venture with her to oblivion
or return to the warm and grow old?

REDISCOVERY

As a boy, I was led by hedges, trees and leaves
down country lanes where tractor traffic could be heard far off,
so ample warning was given to us in the road,
whether tar-bubble popping or throwing rubber balls.
Mostly in the orchards, we raced and climbed up high,
where we saw abandoned birds' nests, with pips inside,
where we scrumped the early unripe apples, plums and pears,
after we'd sated ourselves on the long grass's hidden windfalls.

In youth, when the lanes were blossomed as I did too,
I graduated to the ladders and wire branch hooks,
filling the baskets belted to the waist, and, muscles flexed,
moved ladders for the headscarfed women in the topmost bough.
I did not know how such things seeped into the soul,
and so, through thirty years of houses, family and work,
they were things to look at, to visit and admire,
to talk with friends about what nature was and why and how.

But later, finding love that heightens every sense and nerve,
I found myself in a town garden inside a brick Victorian wall,
and, without awareness or belief, I found myself led on again
to see each bush and tree, each single bud and burgeoning flower,
as something that had been given back to me.
The primroses and the bluebells, violets and daisies too,
of my small patch of countryside, they merged my life together,
as if I'd hardly been away from them for just an hour.

Only now I see and feel them with the whole of this real me,
not with the half-awakening of one newly in this world,
but with awareness of knowing that when something's gone,
(three decades' absence since I lost touch with earth,)
that I'd missed out perhaps on something of myself inside.
And yet what I feel when now I see and touch and smell,
is the sheer joy of recovering something you thought was gone,
revelling in the sensuousness of a mutual rebirth.

SECTION D –
PEOPLE AND FRIENDS

ON A FRIEND MUCH MISSED

As we drive away from the house where he no more lives,
thoughts of him fill my head as always, as they did.
His still grieving widow waves and as she gives
her final smile, we turn the corner – now she's hid.
My sorrow in matching hers cannot come near,
for hers has more than half of her but left;
but when into the empty gap in my life left I peer,
my watery eyes betray how much I'm still bereft.

Why do some losses on our hearts they take such toll
and regularly take us back again over well trodden ground,
while others, while they temporarily our spirits dull,
become recorded in our heads as part of one's life's round?
They must have had something beyond us to define,
that their memory upon our hearts keeps such a hold.
Will I ever have such grip upon their memories of mine?
My friend no longer fears such things – but I grow old.

A DAY FOR HIM

He would have loved a day like this.
I can see him in the heat – in bliss! -
with only a singlet on his upper half
and overalls rolled up to the calf,
grappling with some job to build or paint,
a straightforward task at home or quaint
and quirky customer's request. All one to John!
Or tinkering with a bike he's working on,
wiping up both the oil that drips down on the floor,
as well as the sweat that down his face does pour.

John, it is not fair this world goes on without you.
It ought to stop at least an hour or two;
and so it does for many of us who care
and think you should be with us here to share
such moments day by day and year on year.
Please hear this from all who hold you dear -
death stole you from us against our will;
but those that loved you, they do so still.

A MAN LIKE HIM

Life's given him plenty of kickings, but he never says, 'Poor me!'
He seems to draw on an endless store of positivity
towards the very many things that would knock most people flat.
Now-you have to be proud to know a man like that.

No one could blame him, breathless, if he sometimes felt like sliding
Into some kind of ditch of despair about what life's providing.
When his chances of being completely fit are, shall we say, somewhat slim,
now – you have to be proud to have a friend like him.

Of course he has his blessings, notably a lasting love
who stands beside him, trying to shield him from those blows above;
but essentially he's the man he is, always has been, his own.
Now - you have to be proud that he's someone you've known.

And if he goes before me, and I don't say he may,
it'll be etched upon my mind's screen until my dying day
that he was someone in my life who did as we all should,
who lived life's ups between its downs and found them - pretty good!
With half his joints removed, replaced, an iffy heart-through it all,
he seems to rise above it, makes his mark - that's our friend, Paul.

THE PIANO

It sits, this box of darkly grained and polished wood,
with ornaments on top the closed lid, even a stain
where once a cup
was tipped up,
and coffee set and dried, leaving a greyish circle
on which even studied rubbing worked in vain.

In its centre is a second lid, which has a key -
the key to other worlds that cause this room to vanish.
When this lid's lifted,
this world has shifted
on its axis this domesticity secure
to where he, as ruler, can all doubts banish.

Such power! As in its thrall, he forces all things from his path,
and makes the road ahead seem ominously clear.
All doubts are curbed,
as, undisturbed,
he moves through darkness, crashing storms and threats;
his fingers driven by the music's fear.

But comes a pause and then, like one in passion's ecstasy,
with tender touch of fingers finding secret places,
the pleasure surges,
fulfilling urges,
and dreams float lightly through this whole new life,
and a thousand smiles light up a thousand faces.

And when at last, post passion spent, he rises from the stool.
The lid is closed; the entrance to his inner soul
is now concealed,
its secret sealed,
and it is just a piece of furniture once more -
until again his touch stirs it to life, and makes him whole.

PLAYING FOR LIFE

Amidst routines with which he's tasked,
a something he'd thought forgotten stirs inside,
like a childhood memory that comes to you unasked,
and, unknowing, he is led into the other room.
He feels the pull
and moves the stool
into its place, and, almost unaware, finds his fingers
moving across those keys so smooth and yielding;
heartbeats hasten, but hands' memory lingers
as they start him on a journey to – somewhere .
Already he feels the beauty, as everything flows
across the keyboard, mind and body, hands and heart.
He knows that he must get this right – 'Here's how it goes!'
– and now he's through – and recognises with every fibre
the basic urges
the blood's old surges
which pull him through that so familiar door
into a place which is both strange yet old,
making him know he has been here before.

Then comes release, like calmness after storm;
this world is his and his alone, in almost painful peace;
nothing and no one else exists in this new norm.
While his soul sleeps,
the music sweeps
away the obstacles that otherwise might block the trail.
Nothing to hold him now; he has no choice -
within a finger's touching distance of some holy grail –
only a faulty key's vibration could ever halt him.

And then it's done-his fingers rest, he feels them strained.
Tiredly yet exultantly, he shuffles the sheets he sees
and, trying to rise, he finds his body strangely drained
of all the energy he's ever had or could have;
though his body's tired,
his soul's been fired,
and as he moves back into that first room for tea,
to converse perhaps on matters he must now allow as real,
he knows he's stored another piece no one can ever see
of what makes sense of why he lives at all.
Has he just had his glimpse of what we all, since birth,
have wondered why we're placed here on this earth?

HOW MANY?

'HOW MANY GRANDCHILDREN HAVE YOU TWO GOT?'
'Twelve altogether – and yes, it's a lot!'
'BUT DIDN'T ONE DIE? THAT WAS SO SAD;
AND WASN'T HE JUST A SIX YEAR OLD LAD?'
'Yes, he did, and we count him, you see,
Because six years old is what he'll always be.'
'BUT WHAT ABOUT ONE GIRL WHO HAS NOT
    ONE OF YOUR GENE?'
'That's not the point. You must see what I mean.
She's as much one of ours, just like any other,
We love her as much as her sister and mother.'
'WELL, ONE OTHER QUESTION, SO I CAN BE SURE;
WHICH ONES ARE YOUR HUSBAND'S AND
    WHICH ONES ARE YOUR?'
'I don't understand such a question you ask;
and, frankly, I need to take you to task.
You're judging and measuring things by the law,
Children are not things that are bought in a store.
There's only one law that applies in this case,
And that's the law of love of the whole human race.
No one owns anyone in our family,
We love them all equally, till the day that they're free,
free to live their lives and go their own ways;
and after, they'll still be loved for the rest of our days.

AN IMPOSSIBLE PAIRING

So difficult when they're together – impossible to be apart;
are they opposite poles or two parts of one heart?
Shouting and fighting in the earlier phase
highlighting the problems of those greener days.
And so they parted, each for their own affair,
pretending, self-deluding, their fate lay elsewhere.
Yet inside lurked a flame though burning low,
not quite extinguished, still simmering slow.
When those affairs ended, you could see in their eyes,
lay the realisation all that had been lies.
Like some magnet pulling them towards their fate,
each of them wondering – was it too late?'
They had love around them, from such as me and mine,
but we were all helpless; we're no power divine.
But perhaps there's been help, perhaps from above,
we can and do believe in the power of love.
Some force has caught them and brought them back here,
it may help them through any new troubles to steer;
they can fight it in vain if things should go wrong,
but what is between them will prove much too strong.
They were meant for each other, whatever their ways,
perhaps they'll carry on loving till their dying days.

THE INVISIBLE WALL

Such memories we've shared; now I carry hers too.
Some days of long ago, she can just sometimes find
and I seize upon them so keenly, just like a blind
man grasping at some familiar post trying to make sure
that he can reach that place in which he feels secure.

I reach out for her, my love, and feel that she's still there,
but when I search for her, the core I know, the centre,
she's gone into that place of hers, the one I cannot enter.
Her smiles remain, just like the ones we both recall,
but now they hide her other self, behind this invisible wall.

Those memories! I feast upon them every single day,
helping me to prompt her through daily routines,
taking comfort in the safety of our familiar scenes.
Almost guiltily, I seek solace in my faith, and pray
that tomorrow be no worse than yesterday.

I know the real she's hiding there, behind that unseen wall
and think she knows it too through faith we've shared.
Somewhere beyond this life, the one we've had while paired,
the two of us we'll be united, joined invisibly at the heart,
nothing, no invisible wall, to keep us two apart.

AFTER YEARS OF TEARS

Today she spoke – or rather sang-
just a few words from 'The Messiah'-
but in those sounds all memories rang
and thirteen years were swept away.

Near deaf to me for all those years,
behind dementia's solid wall,
and lately too her body showed fears
of losing the battle for her soul.

And now! – if only for a moment or three,
we reunited in our mutual bond,
and I could only weep for her and me
in knowing love's always been there.

Not that love that's tenderness and care,
that 'looking after', vitally, gladly given,
but the love that only two of us can share –
for that I wept, that it was found again.

A MUSICAL REUNION

Finding choral music as a mutual passion,
soon after their first youthful meeting,
his spirit then became attuned to hers,
and their affection soon was more than fleeting.

Through many years of airs and hymns,
requiems, psalms and sometimes simple song,
whilst they shared aloud in the choirs and choruses,
underneath souls were singing, 'With you I belong'.

Then passing years of family and homes
brought those human periods of joy and pain,
but beneath the noise of life's vicissitudes,
they could hear the quietness of their own refrain-
the one that told them through an inner voice
reassuring them both that,whatever the hour,
they had each other, he she, she he,
and beyond themselves, perhaps a greater power.

Then tragically deafness fell upon her mind,
building a sightless wall across their love-linked way
so that, enduring years of demential hell,
he listened – could not hear, until – one day!-

she suddenly sang those few words from Messiah,
then, falteringly, from 'Jerusalem', and so he wept,
knowing now, through that tormented time,
musical memory had their love together kept.

WITHOUT DEATH

'Without death, there is no life.'
These words I say to myself as another call comes,
asking me to speak at a dear friend's funeral.
'You do it so well.' 'They loved you so much.'
And I did
And so I do.
And I am left to dwell upon the life that now is not
of another fellow friend
who's reached their end.

Today we celebrate lost lives at these occasions
And so I do – and play my part.
Yet when I'm home and think of him or her,
how can I celebrate that their unique stays
upon this earth
right from their birth
have cruelly ceased to be and they live only in my mind.

And so I weep for them, each one.
The talk is always of how he or she will cope
without the one that's gone.
But I reach out sometimes for that departed one,
and try to reach and grasp them
staring at photos of them in my life
that somehow, unfairly, still is.

I tend not to dwell on when I'll be the next.
Oddly, my love for them keeps me alive
as much as them–and yet – !
I'm sure my younger selves who praise me
for my bringing them to life as laid to rest
may think and wonder who will speak
when the necessary time arrives!

SOMETHING IN THE AIR

(A FAMILY WEDDING)

A panoply of pink and purple,
a pastel paradise, it seemed,
seeing the men in their pale blue suits
and the women in their flowery, flouncy dresses;
all of this formed a backcloth
to the rural setting for this special day.

The grey clouds hovered, as if they dared to intervene,
but were thwarted by some mysterious force.
This essence permeated through the day,
and I wondered what it was.
What was it that lit up that day,
that spread around us and above?
Until it dawned upon me for us all –
it was Dominic's and Phoebe's love!

REALLY GONE?

And are they really gone for good?
These ones I worked with years ago,
and even laughed and played with in that time.
For when I'm told this one has died,
that one's no more,
and another's passed away,
I rely upon the messenger,
yet still I am not sure.

Those friends I've loved and seen them leave,
and even spoken for them at their end,
I grieve for them and weep for them,
and cover the gap in my minused life
with photos, reminiscences and love,
and sharing these with those they've left behind.

But that those others really are not here
I cannot grasp – for they must live.
So Bob's still fifty three
and George is forty nine
and youthhood's Carol is merely twenty five.
Why should I believe this idle chat
that distorts all my memories?
They must still be there, within my head and heart,
as vivid as they've always been –
for if I let them go, then part of me goes too,
and leaves me nearer to that very fate
– the one that I refuse to them.

A DEATH IN DECEMBER

He died in December –
now I'll always remember
that time of the year with a kind of fear;
for while the world is calling out 'Christmas is near',
and we're all supposed to be filled with good cheer,
I feel welling up in my eyes just a tear
for I can't help but remember
that he died in December.

Where once there was him, there's a space;
where once was his voice there's no sound.
I listen in vain for him calling my name;
I close my eyes and feel his arms round.

There can be family treats due in December,
like birthdays, weddings, even birth,
but raising a glass or a laugh or a smile
can seem as hollow as 'Peace on earth'.

There'll be no peace on earth for me now
not at this time in December.
They say it's better you know to let the tears flow
and let yourself always remember
that though he's not here to say, 'Happy New Year!'
maybe he's just gone ahead?

So try to remember each himless December,
that you keep him alive when you remember .
Although cruelly taken, this month can awaken
the best thoughts and memories you've got
and don't be afraid-he can hear what you say-
when you come to the actual December day,
to tell him, 'We still love you a lot!'

REFLECTIONS ON HEARING
OF A DEATH

It seemed fitting that it should be at dusk
when I heard the news that Bill had died.
I sit outside afterwards and listen to the silence
of a world without him,
watching a breath of evening air moving caressingly
through the honeysuckle while I muse,
gently brushing the hollyhocks,
each receiving its mini shocks,
as if they'd also heard the news.

I dare not close my eyes in case I hear
Bill's painful struggle with each single breath.
while these ones so unfairly move across the grass,
filling its lungs and mine with scent and colour.
And I sit and think of other dear friends gone,
but also of those who seem to smile through every tear,
who hold each moment that they have so dear,
and I am privileged that I can with them share
such time together breathing the same air,
never knowing if or when will be the last-
but does it matter? The present soon is past.

Perhaps we should not ask for more
but of course we always do for sure,
fearing that this honeysuckle might be the last
      we savour
or the buddleia cluster might have lost its flavour
for the mass of bees that hover and explore it now.

I wish I could have put at least one foot in his door
to stop its final closing in on him,
but that a door will one day close on all of us
is the one thing of which we can be sure.
But one thing I can't know, and now I never will-
whether he knew my life was richer for knowing Bill.

LAST EYE OPENING

She'd stayed asleep when I last visited,
while I chatted with her family there;
but as I kissed her wrinkled hand
as I rose to say goodbye,
her eyes opened
and although they didn't know me,
I saw them and knew her again.

Then, walking home, I saw again her smile
and I recalled our chats –
of family and travel
and especially that blue Canadian lake -
of flowers and colours, of hopes and fears
and all those things that make up all our lives,
for she was, like you and me,
someone of real worth.

A few days later came the call
that 'Dot has passed. The end was peaceful
and her family there.'
And though I knew that it was due,
nothing prevents the surge of grief
that sweeps moistly over you
softened only by belief
that she'd been greatly loved.
But she's still here,
locked forever in my memory's store,
and though when that store's opened,
the best is what had gone before,
I would not have missed that last eye opening,
for, though she did not see,
they made complete
her time with me.

REMEMBERING MICHAEL

Four years ago, we waved him on his way, in the manner that
    he'd asked of us,
with smiles and jokes - sadness hidden as bidden
– with after-glasses clinked, and his favourite puddings
    downed in their familiar restaurant.
Yet he stays in our memories, kept in the albums of our lives,
which we take out either when we choose to sit and open at that page,
or when some trifling incident pushes unasked into a busy day,
when we are forced to stop, perhaps hold back a tear,
or even rage against the injustice of the card that he was dealt.
Such rage comes all from us, not him who turned it over, saw its say,
and faced it like the man he was – he knew no other way –
with wit, with calm, and careful preparation for that then very future day.

So here we sit; we talk of him and hold him in our hearts and mind;
our anecdotes seem to keep him living as if here today.
And yet – some parts of him we cannot reach;
    disrespectful would it be to try;
they lie within the souls of those who loved him most – and there they'll stay.

TAMMY

There's a big hole left in a lot of lives just now -
left by our Tammy – daughter, sister and aunt.
Why she had to leave us, we can't work out how -
maybe some can make sense of it – I know I can't.
But she's not really gone; we can still hear her voice,
laughing out loud, shattering any peace.
Her family's memories will eventually rejoice
when they think how she loved each dear nephew and niece.
We're proud to have known her, and we loved her too –
such positivity-near too good to be true.
Even when her speech muddled and her words got stuck,
she'd laugh it all off – God, I loved her pluck!
Ah, Tammy, we'll miss you! Forget you? Never!
You're engraved in our minds and our hearts for ever!

PATRICK

I sometimes felt I'd known him in his youth.
The smile always at the corner of his mouth
made me see him sitting and seeing,
then saying of that girl, 'She's meant for me!'
And so she was;
he was right because
together they made the one we all knew-
'Pat and Sylvia' through and through.
When we shook hands, I seemed to feel
his holding a grandchild in his other hand
or offering a drink to all
while he threw back his head to laugh.

And now they are both gone, that he and that youthful one;
I won't know for sure that I was right,
and yet I do, because of him still being here in her.
I weep for him. I weep for her.
I weep for me for what I'll never see;
I weep for all of us for what one day we'll be.
I cling to love – he had it – he still has it –
I hope you all do too.

OUR JENNY

So she's now gone – our Jenny Wren;
we'll never see her like again.
She's left the stage for evermore-
no use our calling out 'Encore!'

But close your eyes and you'll see her now
coming on stage for that final bow.
You'll hear her voice, accents unique,
holding the audience as she starts to speak.
At rehearsals, rising above the rest,
glaring at anyone giving less than best!

Ah, Jenny Wren, you had such flair.
It's hard to think you won't be there!
We love you – we miss you. Forget you? Never!
You're performing in our hearts for ever.

SECTION E – STILL LOVING

WHO KNOWS?

Perhaps you and I passed in the street so many years ago?
Perhaps you got off the bus as I got on?
Perhaps, with others on our arms, we didn't even look to see
if that passer-by was worth consideration.
We'll never know for certain.
But this I do know now –
that that bad luck which kept you from my gaze and arms
was simply a disguise for what we might call a blessing.
For our luck changed when later years found that chance
this time had got it right, and threw us in each other's path.
Who knows our luck if earlier fate had done that trick?
It matters not, as surpassing what we have now would be -impossible-
and way beyond what any kind of luck could bring.

AN UNEXPECTED MEETING

(JUNE 11TH 2020)

Hat pulled slightly down across her head, she skipped
along the road, around the bend, across the park.
The rain began to fall-she felt her shoulders dampen
as the drops got heavier and the sky grew dark.

Some way off, she saw a man moving unhurriedly her way,
carrying an umbrella as if prepared to walk a mile.
His oddly reassuring bulk gave her heart a kind of jolt,
and its convulsions spread towards her face, making it smile.

As she neared him, that smile seemed of its own will to grow;
her step quickened, and so did his, it seemed.
Surely, she couldn't know and yet somehow she did;
the rain now stopped and her damp garments steamed.

The nearer he came-the more certain she became.
Impossibly, he'd be the one with whom she'd spend her life!
As they closed, his hand engulfed her clammy glove with love-
no words, for thirty years she's loved him as his wife!

LASTING

She had thought it possible that love might fade
when domesticity cloaked its secret skin.
She feared that passion might expose itself
as mere crude fleshiness when love grew thin.
as flimsy thin as the clothes removed in urgency.
She worried that the cracks in her own face
could be the breeding ground for the germs of something
that might destroy the certainties of what they had.
She had been certain in gateways on Summer evenings
or in the backs of cars on wintry nights,
when the lights from the nearby houses
formed the backdrop to their mutual passion.

But there were things she had not known.
She found that love lay in the quickening of returning steps
after simple shopping expeditions,
or eating ready meals for two by the fireside's heat.
She found her certainty renewed in coffee in a public place
and his love engulfing her in their staring face to face.
His hand engulfing hers for eternity - and more -
held the same passion as anything they'd had before.

YOUNG LOVERS

I wonder what they will do when they find real love?
And how will they know that this is real?
Hooked by eyes' and bodies' nets,
they've loved and lost, noted the dates
when they came round to rub the soreness of a memory still raw,
sometimes that only made them miss that someone more.

How can they know, when life sets mirrors all around
that seem to show the real thing when you look,
only to find that what they thought was just like in a book
was in fact a catchy tune made up of empty sound?

Only when you look through the filter of that other's eyes
and see yourself as well, can you realise
that your world is part of other worlds and every day
gives you the chance to healthily neglect, and in that way
you find each other to be the one you can release,
when, being apart a while, you know you're both at peace.

THIS PIECE OF CORN

This piece of corn I took it from your hair;
And when I took it from your hair,
I took your eyes and mouth and there
I placed you in my car.

This piece of corn I took it from your hair
And when I took it from your hair,
I took that day, that sun, that field and there
I placed them in my car.

And there we share our journeys now,
I and the inner you, the secret I can touch,
sometimes through body, sometimes soul.
So, as you move through daily life
in its mundane ways and chores,
don't be surprised sometimes
to feel a shock,
a tingle, or a surge of need.

It is only I who love you,
As I take this piece of corn from out your hair.

DON'T CRY

What tears are these
tensing at the surface of your eyes?
What voice or tone
has been the point to pierce the well
of that vulnerability
deep inside you?

Don't be afraid.
The warmth of the love I have for you
will dry up every source or spring
and turn your tears to condensation
on the windows
through which the two of us
can look out on all the world
past and present
and we are safe inside
to see the future.

THE NEW BELIEVER

I see the churchgoers solidly set off for Christmas songs,
Some tutting at the folly of seasonal side shows.
A few are smug, but all are snug.
Something inner warms them against the wintry blows.

These certain people hug their rituals deep inside;
Similarly I feel their certainty so fine.
I am content with what's been sent
not from above, but your hand in mine.

Surrounded by that mix of folly and general cheer,
for some this season holds a certainty that's willed.
Our love is mine: like Christmas wine,
drunk and yet so constantly refilled.

So thanks, my love, you brought me a belief
which sustains me now, through warmth and cold.
Better than eternal is flesh and blood here now,
because my god and I together we grow old.

ASHES AND ASHES

Today she did not talk to his ashes
and she felt guilty.
'It's not that I love you less
or forget in any way what we were.
But the bright Autumn sun caught me unawares
by bouncing off the hedge's leaves
distracting me to follow the yellows and oranges
in one long lingering row of motion.
The browns and reds were drawing me back to life,
a life without your warm solidity,
but I don't want to go -
I am not ready yet.'

The ashes could be anything, I suppose.
Their greyness says it all.
But they show him sitting under that tree,
hat pulled forward,
eyes closed,
mind open wide,
perhaps a picture forming its readiness for pen or brush.
And so, I must take the tree's branch
and have it carved into a casket,
a bed inside which these ashes lie,
secure against the world and time-
and where our love cannot be sifted out.

Although I daily learn of life without him
while I see the winter bareness of his tree,
I need to find a resting place
for the love I still had left to give when he left.
And though I will not hurry to my end
because he taught me how life must be held,
I need a peace within my grasp.
So another branch I need to shape
into a bed for my greyness when it comes,
leaving me free to feel the sun till then,
when we will lie side by side inside
till all the wood and trees merge into one.

AN ANNIVERSARY SONNET

What an unimagined thrill it was to fall in love for real
find that strange affinity in body, mind and soul.
The passion of those early years made us one whole,
on which serenity of later times might place its seal.
Strange it is throughout this time, as we both age,
how we grow closer, me the tree, you entwining rose,
while each one new parts of us to the other shows,
this newness only fascinates us more on each new page.
In voluntary isolation, bound together twenty-four seven,
as a work of art, once well-loved and then a while neglected,
shows us facets often hitherto unseen or unsuspected,
each day we find fresh sameness in our purpose-built heaven.
So it is, that each new you and new me continually discovers
that we two, this day, remain our first and last and only lovers.

I WONDER IF SHE KNOWS

We look at the photos together
and note with some satisfied pleasure
how little we've changed
at least outside.
Beneath we've both grown
in so many ways,
I know that we both know.

I gaze at her beauty often
and marvel that so many years
have made so little difference
at least outside.
Beneath she has changed
yet still stayed the same,
I know she knows I know.

I wonder if she knows
that her beauty lies beneath,
that under her flawless skin
lies a spirit
that's gentle but stirring
in so many ways.
She doesn't know that I know.

I wonder if she knows
that I'm in love with what's beneath,
even if her skin were wrinkled,
fingers bloated,
body gnarled,
in so many ways.
I'm not sure that she knows!

HIDDEN AND NOT

I look at my unattractive feet
with their wrinkles, lumps, dark veins and marks,
and strangely remember how I loathed my father's,
as an immature, age-unaware eyed lad,
and he still short of my years now.
But then I see her still beauty bounce,
shining eyes, sad-faced smile for me,
refreshed dress twirling above toes so free-
perhaps the rest of me is not so bad!
So, while we both have ageing parts to hide from view,
the ones we show the world are just as real;
that something deep inside we've shared this while
is pushing outwards to make our bodies smile!

OLDER AND STILL

Although we both are older,
me grey and you more prone to sleep,
we still can both take hold the day
and shape it to our will.
So we can keep what we have always had
and bend it this way or that until
it looks just as our loving art requires.
Those looking in or on can only guess
at what we did when we set out on our creation.
But we are not finished yet-oh, no!
there are fine touches to be made and, yes,
small pieces still to put in place as we shall strive
towards some near-perfection whilst alive.
Yet, if arrived, there'd be no kind of art's re-birth,
since what we've always had was strictly of this earth.

WITHOUT YOU

Sometimes in our most passionate hours
when we believe the whole world is ours
it can sweep over me
where might I be
if I ever were – without you.

When we walk hand in hand in a crowded street
and as a couple we meet and greet
if your hand should slip
one day from my grip
I'd be on my own – without you.

When we separate for an hour, three or four,
and know the joy of meeting once more,
if one day you're not there,
I'll know only despair,
I'd be standing there – without you.

When we dance together, arms entwined,
and the sense of your body fills my soul and mind,
when the music's left
and my arms bereft,
I'll be just empty – without you.

And in our house, each in our own part
with the distance joining us at the heart,
if you weren't in your room,
my room is just gloom,
I'd be in my place – without you.

And when one day, one of us must leave,
something we now both refuse to believe,
I'll be lying as dead
on my single bed,
whichever it is, I'll be – without you.

SECTION F – FROM THE NURSING HOME AND HOPE CENTRE

(NOTE: this first poem is not really my poem at all – it belongs to a group of residents in Symphony Nursing Home in Northampton where I asked them for some of their most cherished memories and then put them together in this piece. It is thus really their poem.)

MEMORIES OF OUR FAVOURITE THINGS

The things that we've loved they do not disappear;
in the back of our minds, they are always still here.
The pleasures, even sad ones, that they gave are real
and when we close our eyes, we see and we feel
these things from the past------------ and they last!

So, close your eyes, but leave open your nose
to recapture the fragrance of lavender and rose;
You can almost smell its colour, orange, yellow or red;
while from the oven comes the smell of fresh bread.

Now close your eyes, but leave open your ear
and back from the past comes these things they hear-
the lapping of water against the keel of the boat,
while he sits there, book in hand, the canal afloat;
a glass of wine completes this remembered scene,
while above, the birds sing, what does it all mean?
Does it mean the past's gone, never to return?
No, it's still there when your mind and heart yearn.
Again, close your eyes, and you're again in that place
when the seaspray falls in drops on your face.
Can you taste the salt there? Is your heart aching
to see once again those remembered waves breaking?

Now close your eyes, your body feels the thrill
of cycling to school the first time, up, downhill.
A rickety bike – you fell off – scars and graze!
But nothing removes the joy of those days.

Schools hold such memories for just about all,
gathering together in some dusty hall,
your class photo taken with the head, a Miss Wing,
she remembers so clearly, not missing a thing.

On Monday mornings, the scent of an empty room,
dry and dusty it stays until along comes a broom
to sweep it away at least for a while
though nothing takes away, as she tells it, her smile.
He remembers the second day more than the first,
crossing your legs, almost fit to burst,
Getting lost, the wrong class, can no one help out?
You'll never forget these, of that we can't doubt.

Again close your eyes, and you'll feel in your hand,
a shiny new snooker cue, with one small brass band,
pointing you to somewhere a few years back,
you still feel the thrill as you potted that black!

Each moment's unique, each one like no other,
as special to each one of us like a father or mother,
like finding that hen's egg out in the field,
picking it up gently so the shell doesn't yield,
you can still feel the thing warm in your hand,
some freckled, some white-and all straight from the land!

Once again close your eyes and you'll feel all the cold
of snow on your hands and wet on your feet
Woolly gloves, woolly socks, all soaking wet,
drying by the fire, as close as we can get,
watching the steam rise as it dries out the rain,
while Mum mutters something about a chilblain!

Ah, open fires! What memories for all
before central heating warmed each floor and wall.
You could stare in the flames and see whole worlds there,
lost in our dreams-like the ones we now share.

TWO HOMES

(SONNET FOR SYMPHONY HOUSE)

I have two homes, where I am quite at rest;
In both, I feel at ease, happy to take what others give.
The first is all around me here, carefully created like a nest;
the other is in my head and heart, the one in which I used to live.
This one fulfils me, so I'm glad to wake each morrow,
receiving nothing but kindness, friendliness and care.
The other is just as real but slightly tinged with sorrow
that those I shared it with can be no longer there.
Sometimes in the comfort of an afternoon chair,
I close my eyes and have the best of both these places.
The reality of this home and the one that once was there
merge with the picture of those so familiar faces,
that sometimes I feel running down my cheek a tear,
knowing that the difference is- YOU are not here.

I MISS HIM

I miss him and it always makes me feel so sad,
when I think about the years together that we had.
We stayed together all that time, through smile and tear-
we drove each other mad at times, my dear!
And yet I always wanted you to be at home with me;
we'd put the kettle on and settle down to tea.
The place we lived in, when it was just we two,
became the third one, part of me and you.
Losing you was something I had not foreseen-
I'd hoped it could stay as it had always been.

And then our home it had to go, soon after I was left alone;
I knew that I could not manage on my own.
The people here are kind and sweet, both residents and staff,
but secretly, I'm not really here, just a half -
half of a couple, which when I close my eyes,
I am part of again, till waking then, I realise,
that you're not here; day passes day, week passes week-
that's why you see this tear roll down this cheek.

DREAMING AT SYMPHONY

I close my eyes in this so comfortable chair;
the room is filled with pleasant murmurs in the air.
Here we are, back in this old room of ours;
so many memories we have, of joys and cares.
I recall some rainy days you went out to come back,
a pot of tea we shared, whilst drying out your mack!
Sometimes, I was the one who went out and returned,
I knew it was my coming back for which we yearned.
Mostly we were together in those latter years,
perhaps I should have told you more about my fears
that one day, you'd go and stay away for ever;
it is still hard to know that your return is –never!
Suddenly I wake and realise I'd dosed;
a nurse approaches with some tea; I'd just supposed
all that before, and still I 'm really only half here,
half in this home of Symphony and half in the old place dear.
This place is friendly, warm like a fire's ember,
yet each day helps me to remember
that I need not worry if I fall asleep,
there are many here who'll help me always keep
my present self safe, yet they let me know
that if back into my old life I want to go,
I can nod off, go back and need not fear;
though you are gone, yet both of us are here.

LOVE AND FRIENDSHIP

I often saw them sitting and chatting together
and wondered what each of the other one thought.
One all smiles and forgiveness,
the other quite terse, sometimes quick to find fault.
But of the faces we show to the rest of the world,
On what's behind them, can a light be shone?
Perhaps only a soulmate can see underneath-
the smiles still has hers-the other now gone.
They seemed so mismatched, but they chatted for ages,
unaware that for one, life was closing its pages.

We saw her two hours before she died;
we kissed her goodbye, said we'd see her tomorrow.
She gave us a smile and thanked us for coming,
with really no hint of the imminent sorrow.
But that smile later told me what I should have known,
that, beyond the horizons of the human heart,
love has no boundaries, limits or rules,
love keeps us together, even when we're to part.

ENDURING LOVE

I'm shown the photographs in her personal room,
some black and white, some framed, some spare.
A wedding shot shows a young pair, the handsome groom
and bride smiling with so much to share.
I see her beauty in a photo at a formal dance,
then pictures of their daughters, smiling down.
These girls, now women, I look at them askance-
the handsome family man, femininity all around!
I see him now, still handsome and alert;
to all of us she's lost to him, but yet I dare
to say his love for her outlasts the grievous hurt.
He sees and loves her inner self-he knows she is still there.
When I ask what can he do – and when and how-
he says, 'She did so much for me; it's my turn now.'

A VISIT TO THE NURSING HOME

I visit elderly folk in their different states,
Dot, Gloria, Wendy, Barbara and Bill.
'How smart you are!' 'Do come again.'
'Who are you then?' No common refrain.
I say I'll be back and I know that I will;
I'm part of them in our different fates.

How easy it is to think 'they' are the same,
as if all poured from the very same mould,
like the homeless, the poor,
old, jobless and more .
as if having a number of years makes you 'old',
when in fact it's the luck of some game.

These were all once in their different roles,
lovely young women, breakers of hearts,
energetic Romeos, real go-getters,
adventurous couples, trend-setters;
each one in their time has played different parts,
succeeding or failing in some of their goals.

Some have travelled the world in action-packed lives,
sometimes for work, sometimes holiday;
Australia, New Zealand, China, Japan,
India, Canada, even Kazakhstan !
Now such places are memories and as such they stay
stored in the minds of late husbands or wives.

As I leave, I am humbled, and I pause at the gate,
then chat to a passer-by that I meet.
'Visiting a relative? Uncle? Brother?
My Dad died in there, later my mother.'
These words seem to speak to my reluctant feet-
it's time to move on before it's too late.

I need to get home to the here and the now,
to my wife and my home and my books .
Such hard thoughts, my eyes water,
Since just now, life's shorter.
I've learned yet again life's not how it looks-
things to be done before my final bow!

SEVEN AGES OF HOMELESSNESS

First comes the dawning of what is sheer disbelief-
no- this cannot really be happening to me.
Why on earth am I here? I am no bank thief
or murderer- there must be others worse to see?
It can't be true that I'm now on the street this way,
watching those pass who have what I'd got yesterday.

Next comes the outbursts, the rants and the rage.
'It's just not fair; why was it all MY fault?'
I'm raving away like some ham on the stage.
Why pick on me? You all pretend that I brought
it all on myself-I'll get back at you all;
YOU are the reason why I had my fall.

Then comes the depths of deepest despair,
the emptiness, blankness, the vast black pit
that I just stare into-to see nothing there;
I tell myself there's nothing for which I'm fit
but a corner to hide in, somewhere to crawl;
I've nothing to live for – might as well end it all.

Stage four is when into self-pity I'm tempted;
when I look back, I never stood a chance.
My half-full cup has been completely emptied;
the whole world 's been leading me a hell of a dance.
I know I've done wrong, but others have done worse
- why should I be the one who ends up with its curse.

But then comes a stage when glimmers of hope
stop me feeling sorry for myself and I see some sign
that make me question why each day's a long mope;
perhaps not everyone's against me and mine.
A friendly word, a cup of coffee, 'How are you today?'
I can't be all worthless when folk speak that way.

And then from that, perhaps there's resolution.
The help is there; underneath I'm the same;
and in myself it's quite clear, there is the solution.
I can't go back where I was before this all came.
I see now that I had by far the main share
of my troubles and pain that others had to bear.

The final stage is somehow to turn these into action;
with help, I'll tear this blindfold from my eyes
and see those wasted years as just a fraction,
large or small, of the total time I've got, I realise
whether what I've found out about myself is true,
and maybe be of some use to me, the world-and you.

TWO KINDS OF HOMELESS

I read and I rage about the homeless and poor
and I see so many who have to sleep in a door.
Then I read of the rich with their five different places,
the five minute celebs with their orange peel faces
and I'm angry till I realise in one way they're the same;
it's just that they're caught on a treadmill of fame.
Some may have five mansions, but do they have a home?

Home's a place that you're drawn to when too tired to roam;
no matter the cost, style, materials or size,
home isn't a place you judge just by your eyes.
A home is not something you should need to earn.
You walk into somewhere, your heart will turn;
you know it knows you and you've passed its test;
then it wraps itself round you – forget all the rest.
You know you've arrived - no need to roam –
this is your place – this is your home.

THEY SPEAK MY WORDS

(A DRAMA GROUP AT THE HOPE CENTRE)

They don't have much in common with each other;
each one's as individual as any other,
except they've had more than their fair share
of lousy luck in life, sometimes very hard to bear.
Perhaps inside an unwelcoming home, or a school where they felt ignored,
where they learned to just act passively, when really they were bored.
Each of them had a talent, some a lively brain,
but when you get put down so much, you vow not to try again.

Some of them picked the wrong partner, or couldn't kick a habit,
or lost a loved one far too soon, or missed a chance before they could grab it.
Some might have taken a different path, if only there'd been time,
When you spend ages feeling worthless,
you may get attention through crime.

And so the years go slipping by, life looking increasingly dour,
till fate and Hope Centre offer a glimpse of something else,
    if only at first for an hour.
Something that occupies them, their minds ceasing to spin,
and gives them a chance to be someone else, inside that someone else's skin.
For being busy, for a while, in some useful kind of way,
can keep your mind off other things, like questions no one wants to say,
like 'I wonder where I'll sleep tonight?'
    'Why did I get into that fight?'
    'Can I get by without another drink?'
    'When I see them again, what will they think?'

For a couple of hours, engrossed in drama, they adopt a new persona,
a lord or a lady, a compere or a mayor, or even a charity donor.
For a brief spell, all is well, and in me something's stirred,
and I am humbled as they speak my word.
Perhaps we've all had a time in life when we longed to be
    someone other than us?
But with luck and work, we found a way to use what talent
    we had without fuss,
and get some success in our chosen field, always thanking the stars above
that we had the luck to overcome our mistakes and hopefully also find love.

These people we love, they swallow my words,
tasting their meaning for the most part,
and, strangely, I'm the one who feels this in my heart.
Perhaps to them I'm just another of those clever nerds,
but I am still humbled when they speak my words.
And over the weeks, we see different folk emerge
and inside me I feel often a surge
of hope for them all that with those new seeds
of growth that means that their needs
may better be met by the world out there
and through that perhaps there comes better care.
Maybe I'll never know what they got from what I heard
but still I was humbled when they spoke my word.

SECTION G – IN THE WAITING ROOM

A COMING OF AGE

'Please have this seat – this one, just there!'
A young woman's voice rose above the blare
and the bus engine's roar, which, as I heard,
for a split second I thought, 'This is absurd!'
and then I realised – in fact I could see –
it belonged to a woman who was looking at me!

As I flopped in that seat, near another old gent,
I made sure I thanked her as if heaven-sent.
My head's in a whirl; can this really be true
that some young female gave her seat up to you?
I mean – the rule of my youth, so constantly drilled,
was always 'Ladies first' - by my parents instilled.
But, as I sat there, and the rain outside poured,
I knew that the evidence could not now be ignored.
That middle aged man – 'Can you manage that case?'
Those amblers who passed me at my very good pace.
The young ones who smile when I pay with some coin,
and wonder why I look for a queue I can join.

The bus reaches the station – it's in the wrong bay!
I get off with the others — not much more to say.
The world's left me behind; I must face the fact
– there isn't much point in putting on an act.
Well, I'll let it go – we weren't much of a match.
Oh, blast! There goes that other bus I was going to catch!!

TOWARDS THE END OF THE JOURNEY

I boarded the bus of life at birth,
straight from a mother's womb,
little knowing or caring that the final stop
would be my own gaping tomb.

Some of the early stops seemed brief,
hardly pausing before the next,
whole letters and novels were raced through
before I'd scarcely studied the text.

The midway miles felt fresh and free,
passengers joined we quickly knew.
We even felt like singing aloud;
We were a happy crew!

Then a friend of mine got off the bus,
one whom we'd urged to stay;
I don't think till then I'd been aware
how far we were on our way.

My love and I sit side by side,
hands clasped in love and fear
of getting off at different stops,
as the terminus draws near.

I cannot see the driver's face,
and I long to shout, 'Slow down!'
but he powers on regardless
to the edge of this new town.

Now, as the final stop is near,
and I picture a flower-filled urn,
I grow increasingly afraid,
knowing there's no return.

THE SAME OLD STORY

I thought I knew what it was to be old;
after all, I'd seen Grandad and his wife.
They'd seemed to me to be quite contented,
looking back on what they knew of life.

He seemed to live in slippers, a new pair every year,
and his home grown veg were second to none.
Grandma's skill was in crochet and knitting;
they were quiet and they didn't need fun.

Grandad peacefully passed away at a 'very decent age';
everybody, including me, thought he'd done 'pretty fair'.
Grandma lived on in a home for nine years;
I'd always meant to visit her there.

This year, I reached Grandad's 'decent' age,
but I don't feel ready for peace.
I think a lot about my coming end,
hoping for a longer lease.

They may say, 'He was a nice old guy,'
and, 'I was sorry to hear he's passed'.
They'll never know what a coward he was,
scared that each week was his last.

I expect my family will be just the same,
forgetting until it's too late.
By then of course, I'll have gone to 'peace',
on that unavoidable date.

Ah well, it'll be the same for them;
we're all old in our own way.
No one really knows about being old,
Till you get there yourself one day.

AND WHEN I DIE

And when I die, I'll do so knowing,
whatever else my record's showing,
that I've been loved and given love
– out of all proportion.

Blindly, I'd lived with eyes half-closed,
thinking that what I'd had was love supposed
until I found that real love gives, not takes
– it's a real distortion.

I think I might have guessed it changes you,
but I didn't know it changed the whole world too.
I've had to re-think every theory
– and throw away precaution.

No need to worry about what lasts or not;
you know that what it is, you've got.
Each bit of life is up for scrutiny
– it's sheer extortion.

WAITING AT WINDOWS

Have I measured out my life waiting at windows,
watching for the colour of the car to come,
wondering if it will be from this way or that?
Each time I vow that I will wait no more,
but still the windows draw me back.
Perhaps they're offering me some kind of hope,
in forgetting to learn from what the past has taught.
Grandchildren stand on the window seat,
cheering each passing red car,
and noting the sirens and flashing blues,
what a world of endless fun!
If they could see coming down the road
the heartache of those missed appointments,
those broken promises, those dashing hopes,
the gradual draining of the human heart
that follows the early rising of a sunny start,
would they look out with so much glee?
And if I had ever looked out to see
that disappointment is what comes to call,
would those young spectators be here at all?

STILL WAITING

He sits in a kind of bower that he's made
beneath an ancient damson tree and shrouded by bitter sweet jasmine;
the variegated ivy on the Victorian wall completes the frame,
as the Autumn sun filters through and slightly warms his face.
No greater peace seems possible for him
– except of course the one on which he muses
as if it were the Keatsian midnight hour when all seems rich.

So still is he that when his wife finds him, eyes shut,
she thinks – just for a moment – he is gone.
But the still blue eyes open, and as the lit cheeks
crinkle into the kind of smile that she both loves and fears,
she knows he is still just waiting –
waiting for one of his sons
to tell him what he needs to hear.

ON THE ROAD

I'd been on the same road for some time.
Despite a couple of wrong turnings
and a few side roads I'd entered just for fun,
the road still stretched ahead.
Of course I knew where all roads lead
and I hoped before that common end,
the knapsack of my heart might fill
with something other than the weight of its emptiness.
Yet I wondered where my road led.

Then came a chance encounter –
and the journey somehow now seemed different.
My heart was fuller though it was lighter
for my journey now had become the end.

We travelled together from then on
and found peace and excitement were the same,
finding more of me in the more I learned of her.
We found we'd travelled on parallel roads
with similar milestones and some false steps
until somehow the routes had merged
so that we both together knew its end,
though now hoping not to see it soon.

We now know that end is there,
the one as known to all of us
and our only fear is whether
we may not reach it both together.
Yet if it's me that's left to walk the last few steps alone,
I know I won't be, though my movement slows,
for such a love can't end because the body goes.
I'll hobble across my finishing line,
knowing I'll see her once again,
as we walk together down some unknown lane.

STRANGE BUT TRUE

It's strange to know but also true
that, after you've gone, I'll still be loving you.
In fact I'll be more demanding when you're dead,
because I'll need you even more than what I've said.
I'll drink my early morning cup of tea in bed,
forgetting it was I who brought it me instead.
I'll go on the bus with you into town
and check with you the lists we both wrote down.
I'll unlock the door for you on our return
and stand back as you enter while I'll yearn
to brush against you as I can no more
and find I've stood for hours outside the door.

I'll tend the garden's flowers, just for you to see,
while you rest upstairs in your usual place,
and then I'll look above and see your face
as ever at the window, smiling just at me.

In evening, as ever, my head is in a book,
while you'll be elsewhere in the house, both sure
that we're each near – we want no more,
and when we meet we only need our look,
the one that says, 'We're both still here the same.
We didn't dream it – the whole thing was real,
the day we met, the years we had to steal –
that love still burns – our undying flame.'

And, late at night, I'll bring two cups of tea upstairs
and place one each for either side the bed.
I'll see your book open on your side, unread,
and discuss the news with you, the whys, the wheres,
and last, I'll kiss the pillow where you're lying
and check the clocks are set for dawn,
and, probably seeing your mouth suppress a yawn,
I'll turn away, so you won't know I'm crying.

MY TWO WORLDS

I live in my two worlds together,
the present and the past.
One I see with eyes wide open,
the other with them mostly shut.
One is so brief it passes in a flash
and regularly it fails to last
more than a moment before it flows
into that other one and thus that one grows
longer while the other quickly goes.

I carry my past world with me while I live the here and now
and seem to have control of what it might show.
Except that sometimes it decides for me
and I cannot change what was, so quickly does time go .

There is a third world called the future
and I cannot guess its length at all,
although it is much shorter than it once was
when my own past was very small .
Thus as my past gets longer and my future shorter
I see the present as the world I cherish most.
If I have learned from my past world
and can apply it to the here and now,
perhaps my future will be best of all,
– however long or short it will be –
until that time when I only have a past –
and others will have to live the future for me.
Whether they'll ever learn from that
is something I will never know.

Unless of course there is a further world
from where I look and see at last
my followers upon their journey at first long,
until they reach their point of mainly past.
I cannot know about their why or how
for I must focus on what's left for now!

WHEN WE ARE YOUNG

When we are young, the world seems such a simple place,
easy in knowing what's right and wrong.
Just a look sometimes on a parent's face
left us growing up free to help the years along.

As we aged, sometime things seemed less clear;
work, home and family, and all life's other chores
never gave us time to ask, 'Why are we here?'
We knew the rules by other people's laws.

And now, being 'mature', a word preferred to 'old',
there is more time than ever to ponder on that 'Why?'
and as for the answer, when time's as rare as gold,
there's now less time to act, as another year has tolled.

The past can't be redrawn, we have to note with sorrow,
and yet there are two things that we can do with style.
First, grasp on today before it is tomorrow,
Second, keep those memories, they still can make you smile.

THE DAY THE WORLD ENDS

I expect I'll go to get the papers as usual;
after all, there's yesterday still to read about.
I expect the milkman will leave two pints as usual;
after all, he won't know that we will always be 'out'.
I expect I'll pick up some litter on my way to the shops;
after all, might as well keep things tidy to the end.
I might even have my favourite thing for tea that day,
though at what hour the world ends that will depend.

There'll be no time for grand goodbyes,
or tearful partings or tragic speeches;
no time for dwelling on family relations,
which are supposed to touch where nothing else reaches.

I wouldn't call this going out 'with a whimper';
it will just happen and it's best that way
I think myself it's quite a nice way to go,
with a minimum fuss on that particular day.

It won't go down in history because it can't.
History will have gone, like everything past.
Let's just think we've been lucky to have been here at all,
and perhaps made the most of it to the last.
And if we didn't do that, who are we going to blame?
With no future, we'll then only have the past.
We'll leave bills unpaid, debts not recovered;
our only excuse will be the end came so fast.

But no time for regrets – now that's such a good thing,
no time for phrases like 'Ever since the Fall'.
Nothing will matter any more, for any of us.
Perhaps it will be that we were never here at all.

MESSAGE FROM THE DEPARTED

Saying goodbye's always been hard,
but when it's for the final time, words become our ghost;
they seem inadequate, failing us in what we want from them,
choking us when we need them most.
Think of when you woke the morning after we'd had to part
and found that saying goodbye was not the end
for I was still with you in your heart,
our union was simply in another form.

And so, although we can no longer touch,
you'll never cease my presence still to feel,
and when you call to me in dreams at night
I will be there, like a faithful dog coming to heel,
and I am with you when a certain look or smile
perhaps a colour or a smell, a word, cross or kind,
some scene we shared together perhaps
will bring me straight into your mind.
Let that mind sometimes dwell on a moment you recall –
when you and I did this or that together – as one –
such moments cannot ever die,
in them I live with you, until your day is done.

So please remember in the midst of your life now,
that you and I, given the endless span of all human days,
have only taken a short leave of each other
for a while to go our separate ways.
And as you sit somewhere today, perhaps gazing above,
hold on to those moments, for in those you have our love.

----

www.ingramcontent.com/pod-product-compliance
Lightning Source LLC
Chambersburg PA
CBHW051730040426
42447CB00008B/1060